NOTES
WORTH
NOTING

CURRENT ISSUES IN
SERIALS MANAGEMENT

NOTES WORTH NOTING:

Notes Used In AACR2 Serials Cataloging

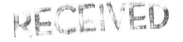
compiled by
Jim E. Cole
Renne Library
Montana State University

and
David E. Griffin
Washington State Library

with the assistance of
Dorothy E. Cole

THE PIERIAN PRESS
1984

Library of Congress Catalog Card Number 84-60637
ISBN 0-87650-181-1

THE PIERIAN PRESS
P.O. Box 1808
Ann Arbor, MI. 48106

Contents

Preface

In 1952 Columbia University Libraries published a booklet by Ruth Schley and Jane B. Davies entitled *Serials Notes Compiled from Library of Congress Cards Issued 1947–April 1951*. This work served as the standard reference source for serials catalogers using both the *Rules for Descriptive Cataloging in the Library of Congress* (Washington, 1949) and later also the first edition of the *Anglo-American Cataloging Rules* (Chicago, 1967), since AACR as originally written closely paralleled the 1949 rules in the description of serials.

With the advent of the second edition of AACR, serials cataloging underwent a great transformation. For example, the description of a serial had previously been based upon the latest issue; now the description was taken from the earliest issue available. When Schley and Davies had compiled their work, all serials were cataloged under their latest title; AACR2 prescribed cataloging under successive title. These and other philosophical and practical changes in the cataloging codes have rendered the Schley/Davies work obsolete, although it is still of use and is indeed a classic in the field.

In 1981 *New Serial Titles* began publishing the complete cataloging record for each serial it listed; in the same year the Library of Congress also began to apply AACR2. This compilation of notes consists entirely of examples derived from AACR2 serials cataloging. The January-November 1981 and January-August 1982 issues of NST have served as the primary source for the notes, augmented by later issues of NST as well as the Serials Supplement to *Monthly Catalog* and additional Library of Congress and CONSER records found in the Washington Library Network database. The examples have been verified on the database, and, when necessary, rechecked in NST. The Library of Congress record number is given following each example so that one may consult the complete cataloging record if desired.

Notes are generally given exactly as found; no attempt has been made to standardize abbreviations, for example, and catalogers should consult Appendix B of AACR2 for prescribed abbreviations. However, two exceptions exist: obvious typographical errors have been corrected, and periods have been consistently omitted after notes ending in a parenthesis, bracket or hyphen.

This book is directed to all serials catalogers and catalog departments using AACR2 for the description of serials. It is arranged by rule number, and thus will serve as a ready reference for a cataloger trying to phrase a note succinctly. Opposing blank pages provide space for recording additional notes. The work may also prove useful to other catalogers as well as to library schools and students.

Jim E. Cole

David E. Griffin

NOTES
WORTH
NOTING

1.7B1. Nature, Scope or Artistic Form of the Item

1. Report to the Florida Legislature and the State Board of Education. [81--640928]

2. A report to the Legislature pursuant to AB 4355, chapter 1170, 1974. [81--642688]

3. At head of title: Annual report to the Governor and the Illinois General Assembly on Public Act 81--202, 1980-- ; Annual joint report to the Governor and the Illinois General Assembly on Public Act 81-202, 1981-- [82-643981]

4. Combined annual reports of agencies which administer Washington State's general government services and pro-- grams. [76--647198]

5. A survey of financial data and management information relative to state agencies and budgetary units. [81-- 644233]

6. A directory of accredited institutions, professionally accredited programs, and candidates for accreditation. [81--641495]

7. A commentary on the state's investment in science and technology. [81--646051]

8. A series of monographs and studies on the history of cartography, reprinted from periodicals since 1800. [68--7512]

9. "Subject, author, and title indexes to books published or exclusively distributed in the United States. Subject and title indexes to current serial publications," cover, 1981. [81--646034]

10. Chiefly tables. [81--649887]

11. ". . . alphabetical list of librarians, heads of library net-- works . . . deans, chairmen of library schools . . . in the United States and Canada" -- Pref. [81--640061]

12. Special bibliography with indexes. [81--643972]

NOTES
1.7B1. Nature, Scope or Artistic Form of the Item

13. Lists stores, companies, executives and buyers in the chain food store market in U.S. and Canada.   [81–649151]

14. Indexes the Society's publications.   [81–649516]

15. Disseminates information concerning new developments and effective actions taken relative to the management of defense systems programs and defense systems acquisition. [81–645840]

16. " . . . bring together publications cataloged by the Research Libraries of the New York Public Library and the Library of Congress . . . " -- Pref.   [81–642144]

17. Schedule covers executive branch of the government. [81–641254]

18. First issue of each year compares first half of current year with first half of previous year; second issue each year compares entire current year with entire previous year. [82–643598]

19. First issue each year devoted to translations into English; the second, into all other languages.   [81–644248]

20. Consists of a selection of the best papers presented at the Association's annual research conference.   [sn82–20268]

21. Some years consist, wholly or in part, of preprints. [sn82–21296]

22. A listing containing all name authority records in the computerized master file at the Library of Congress. [79–647358]

23. Contains articles, outlines, and checklists selected from the Institute's course handbooks.   [81–641156]

24. "Contains all of the judgments of the Saskatchewan Court of Appeal plus selected judgments from other Saskatchewan Courts . . . [and] judgments of the Supreme

NOTES
1.7B1. Nature, Scope or Artistic Form of the Item (cont.)

1.7B1. Nature, Scope or Artistic Form of the Item (cont.)

Court of Canada for cases originating in Saskatchewan" -- P. A--5. [82--642677]

25. Includes annual reports of various institutions. [82--644101]

26. Includes guides to Virginia, North Carolina, South Carolina, Georgia, Florida and the Mississippi and Alabama coasts. [81--644326]

27. "Includes also: Confederate States, U.S. Possessions, Albums and Accessories, comprehensive U.S. Stamp identifier." [80--648769]

28. Issues for 1977-- include also Special list journals being indexed in cooperation with other institutions. Citations from these journals appear in other MEDLARS bibliog-raphies and in MEDLINE, but not in Index medicus. [73--642296]

29. Vol. 1-- based on the proceedings of a series of workshops. [sn82--20071]

1.7B1.   Nature, Scope or Artistic Form of the Item (cont.)

1.7B7. Edition and History

1. Each spring issue also called research ed. [82--640108]

2. At head of title, 1975/76-- committee print. [80--646542]

3. Official ed. [81--642552]

4. Various vols. issued in limited, numbered editions. [82--640432]

NOTES
1.7B7. Edition and History

12.7B1.   Frequency

1. Daily.   [82--641652]

2. Four issues yearly.   [81--640561]

3. Ten no. a year.   [81--641596]

4. Quinquennial.   [81--910358]

5. Two no. each school year.   [82--643235]

6. Occasional.   [81--645093]

7. Irregular.   [81--640579]

8. Monthly (irregular)   [81--643882]

9. Monthly (except July and Aug.) with Nov. and Dec. issues combined.   [sc81--2059]

10. Bimonthly (with additional summer issue)   [81--646174]

11. Monthly, with semiannual cumulations.   [81--641101]

12. Ten monthly issues with two semiannual cumulations. [81--643060]

13. Quarterly, with the last issue being cumulative for the year.   [81--641111]

14. Biweekly, with semiannual references.   [82--642647]

15. Monthly, with annual summary called no. 13.   [79--644001]

16. Vol. 1-- published monthly March through December; Jan./Feb. issue is an annual publication which includes a yearly economic profile.   [sn82--20967]

17. Biweekly during harvesting season, with comprehensive report at end of season.   [gpo82--7013]

18. Three quarterly issues with annual and quinquennial cumulations.   [80--648903]

NOTES
12.7B1.   Frequency

12.7B1.   Frequency (cont.)

19. Nine monthly issues, 3 quarterly cumulations, annual cumulations for four years and a quinquennial in the fifth.   [56–60041]

20. Eight monthly issues, four quarterly issues and annual cumulations which are self--cumulative through periods of five or ten years.   [53--60021]

21. Quarterly (–1967); annual (1968--   )   [81–641164]

22. Quarterly (with additional issue dated Jan.)   ; bimonthly, [81–646318]

23. Biweekly, Feb. 26, 1968--Dec. 9, 1974; semimonthly, Jan. 1, 1975–Sept. 15, 1975; monthly, Oct. 1975-- [81–649133]

24. Monthly,   ; annual,   ; quarterly with annual summary, 1957--   [82–643234]

25. Frequency varies.   [81–643473]

NOTES
12.7B1.   Frequency (cont.)

12.7B2.   Languages

1. In English.   [81--640207]

2. In English and French with separate title pages.   [81--643647]

3. Text in English and French with French text on inverted pages.   [81--645978]

4. English and French,   --1970/76; English, 1976/78-- with summaries in French, German, and Italian.   [81--641147]

5. Articles in English, occasionally in French.   [81--643559]

6. Chiefly Arabic; some English.   [82--642943]

7. In Japanese, with abstracts in English.   [81--649397]

8. Text in Korean, with captions in English.   [sc82--2279]

9. Captions in Japanese and English.   [82--643447]

10. Text in English and German, summaries in both languages.   [81--645745]

11. Summaries in French, German, and Italian.   [81--643245]

12. Summaries in German and Russian; also in English, --1974.   [81--641255]

13. In Portuguese, with the second half of the issue being the English translation.   [82--643575]

14. French or various African languages.   [sc82--3334]

15. Danish, Dutch, English, French, German, and Italian.   [81--640975]

16. Articles are in English, French, German, Italian, Portuguese, etc.   [68--7512]

17. Multilingual, with English translations.   [81--643780]

NOTES
12.7B2. Languages

12.7B2.   Languages (cont.)

18.   Text is multilingual (romanized)   [81–644186]

NOTES
12.7B2. Languages (cont.)

12.7B3. Source of Title Proper

1. Title from cover. [sc82--1213]

2. Title from contents page. [sc82--7551]

3. Title from editorial page. [82--641437]

4. Title from caption. [82--640796]

5. Caption title. [80--649405]

6. Masthead title. [81--643493]

7. Title from portfolio. [81--645221]

8. Title from p. 1 of memorandum. [81--643898]

NOTES
12.7B3.   Source of Title Proper

12.7B4.   Variations of Title

Title Borne by the Serial, Other Than the Title Proper

1. Added title page title: Cadence magazine. [81--640946]

2. Added title page in Latin. [81--640772]

3. Caption title: IEEE control systems magazine. [81--649117]

4. Caption title: Automatizacija poslovanja, Oct.--Dec. 1980. [81--649248]

5. Running title: Estimates, Jamaica. [81--640776]

6. Spine title: AIPG . . . membership directory. [81--640215]

7. Other title: Press, television, radio . . . directory. [sc82--3053]

8. Cover title: Alabama, detailed mortality statistics. [82--643453]

9. Cover title: Market values of taxable real property, 1970--1977 -- Market value of taxable real property, 1978--   [83--640241]

10. Cover title: RS indicadores industriais   -- Indicadores industriais RS   -- Indicadores industriais   [81--641479]

Title Proper

11. Title includes name of incumbent, e.g. Edmund G. Brown, Ronald Reagan. [sc82--7169]

12. Issues for winter 1982-- include a year designation in conjunction with the title, e.g. Morality '82. [82--643724]

13. Title varies slightly. [81--644109]

14. Alternate years have title: Revision of occupational

NOTES
12.7B4. **Variations of Title**

12.7B4.   Variations of Title (cont.)

Title Proper (cont.)

> employment trends in the State of Oregon.   [82–642603]

15.   Alternate issues have title: South African journal for librarianship and information science.   [82–642415]

16.   Order of titles varies.   [82–643935]

17.   Beginning with Sept. 1980 alternate issues are called: Cost engineering newsletter and carry the numbering of the magazine issue preceding it with the addition of an A, e.g., Vol. 22, no. 4 and Vol. 22, no. 4A.   [81–641229]

18.   Some issues lack title.   [82–643960]

Distinctive Titles

19.   Each issue has a distinctive title.   [81–643233]

20.   Some issues have a distinctive title.   [81–643327]

21.   Jan. issue includes a distinctive title: Speakers.   [81–641152]

22.   May issue published as: "Get rich" investment guide.   [81–649093]

23.   Each vol. devoted to a particular subject, i.e. Energetika, toplivo.   [81–645082]

24.   Distinctive title: Decisions of the Civil Aeronautics Board, v. 2, 5 – Economic decisions of the Civil Aeronautics Board, v. 3, 4, 6–12, 14–16 – Safety decisions of the Civil Aeronautics Board, v. 13 – Economic and safety enforcement cases of the Civil Aeronautics Board, v. 17–46 – Economic cases of the Civil Aeronautics Board, v. 47–   [42–38246]

Title Romanized

NOTES

12.7B4. Variations of Title (cont.)

12.7B4. Variations of Title (cont.)

Title Romanized (cont.)

25. Title romanized: Bunkazai chosa hokoku. [82--640851]

NOTES
12.7B4.   Variations of Title (cont.)

12.7B5. Parallel Titles and Other Title Information

Parallel Titles

1. Vols. for −1977 lack parallel title.   [81−645196]

2. Vols. for 1962/64-- lack English title.   [81−641475]

3. Parallel title on cover: Jinhae business directory.
   [81--641768]

Other Title Information

4. "A literary tri--quarterly of the whole art."   [81−646393]

5. "A publication of the government statistical service."
   [81--640828]

6. "Nauchno--issledovatel'skie raboty."   [81−649951]

7. Vols. for 1981/82-- have subtitle: Demand, productivity,
   and population.   [82−642433]

8. At head of title: MP, Jan. 1975−Jan. 1981.   [sn78−789]

9. At head of cover title: Industry report.   [sn83--2074]

12.7B5.   Parallel Titles and Other Title Information

12.7B6. Statements of Responsibility

Corporate Responsibility

1. On cover: Building Cost File Inc.   [81–643051]

2. "Water Resources Division" -- Verso of t.p.   [68–60771]

3. "Office of the Secretary, Assistant Secretary for Public Affairs" – 1980–   [81–643081]

4. Prepared by: Office of Libraries and Learning Tech–nologies.   [81--643691]

5. Prepared and edited by the editorial staff of: Mergers and corporate policy.   [82--642823]

6. Compiled and published by: Economics and Markets Branch, Ministry of Agriculture, Zimbabwe, July--Dec. 1979--   [81–645592]

7. Conferences sponsored by: Secretaria de Industria, Comercio e Turismo, Mato Grosso, Brazil, Aug. 1976-- [82--640127]

8. Sponsored in part by: the Association of Pacific Fisheries. [81–645115]

9. Submitted by: the New Jersey Dept. of Labor and Industry.   [81--641221]

10. Collected by: Office of Management Information. [79--649150]

11. Census conducted by: Idaho State Dept. of Agriculture and the Idaho Crop and Livestock Reporting Service of the U.S. Dept. of Agriculture.   [82--641600]

12. Supported in part by the Association of Academic Health Sciences Library Directors.   [81–640259]

13. "A team of Farm Credit System personnel undertook a project of interpreting and summarizing the annual Food and Agricultural Outlook Conference of the Department of Agriculture."   [82--642878]

12.7B6.   Statements of Responsibility

12.7B6.   Statements of Responsibility (cont.)

Corporate Responsibility (cont.)

14.   Published as a trial research project by the Program Eval--uation Resource Center.   [sc82--8179]

15.   " . . . officially adopted by the Association for Canadian Theatre History."   [82--640492]

16.   "Approved by the World Food and Agricultural Outlook and Situation Board." -- P. 3.   [81--646203]

17.   " . . . from the working files of Berger & Associates Cost Consultants" -- Introd.   [81--641051]

Corporate Responsibility -- Organ, etc.

18.   Official journal of the Deutsche Keramische Gesellschaft. [81--643227]

19.   The organ of: the Shefa Institute for Advanced Studies in Judiasm,   [82--640402]

20.   A publication of the Natural Resources Defense Council. [81--641215]

21.   Official membership roster of: the Nashville Area Cham--ber of Commerce.   [81--643783]

22.   Yearly publication of the congregation of the Mission, and the Daughters of Charity founded by Saint Vincent de Paul.   [81--641811]

23.   Journal of: Direccion de Politicas y Normas, Direccion General de Politica Informatica,   --June 1980; Direccion General de Politica Informatica, Sept. 1980--   [82--643475]

Joint Corporate Responsibility

24.   Issued jointly by: the University of Oklahoma School of Geology and Geophysics and: Stovall Museum of Science

NOTES
12.7B6. Statements of Responsibility (cont.)

Joint Corporate Responsibility (cont.)

and History.   [81–645781]

25. Issued by Schweizerische Gesellschaft fur Ur und Fruh--
     geschichte in cooperation with Verband Schweizerischer
     Kantonsarchaologen . . . [et. al.]   [81–643191]

26. Issued by Agricultural Statistics Unit, with Central Statis--
     tics Office.   [81--641598]

27. Vol. for 1979 issued with: Oficina de Planificacion
     Agricola.   [82--643772]

28. Developed in cooperation with: the State Comprehensive
     Employment and Training Office.   [81–649285]

29. Issued by various divisions of the Office of Operations of
     the Dept. of State.   [64--61222]

30. Sponsored by Region 5, of the Institute of Electrical and
     Electronics Engineers, 1976; and by other sections of the
     Institute, 1977--   [82--642090]

31. Issued by: Staatliche Buchereistelle fur den Regierungs--
     bezirk Freiburg and other state libraries,   ; Staatliche
     Fachstelle fur das Offentliche Bibliothekswesen Freiburg
     and other state libraries,   [81--645108]

32. Vols.   issued by the Centre de documentation scientifique
     et technique, Centre national de la recherche scientifique,
     the Centre scientifique et technique du batiment, and the
     Union technique interprofessionnelle du batiment, Direc--
     tion de la recherche.   [80--647218]

Changes in Corporate Responsibility

33. Issued by: Pennsylvania State Library, Oct. 1963–Mar.
     1971; State Library of Pennsylvania,   [82--641505]

34. Issued by: South Carolina Employment Security Commis--
     sion, Manpower Research and Analysis,   –1978; South

NOTES
12.7B6.   Statements of Responsibility (cont.)

12.7B6.   Statements of Responsibility (cont.)

Changes in Corporate Responsibility (cont.)

>   Carolina Employment Security Commission, Research and
>   Analysis, 1979--   [78--640881]

35.   Issued by: British Museum, State Paper Room, 1967--74;
      British Library, Official Publications Library, 1975--1978;
      and, British Library, Reference Division, 1979--
      [76--647506]

36.   Issued by the Mathematisch--Naturwissenschaftliche
      Klasse; 1880--1917 of the Kaiserliche Akademie der
      Wissenschaften; 1918--1944 of the Akademie der Wissen--
      schaften in Wien; 1945--196 of the Osterreichische
      Akademie der Wissenschaften; and also 1959-- by the
      Verein Osterreichischer Chemiker.   [1--23479]

37.   Issues for   --1970 prepared by the editors of Science and
      electronics and Elementary electronics; 1971-- by the
      editors of Elementary electronics.   [81--641260]

38.   Vols. for Apr. 1980--Oct. 1980 issued by the Economics,
      Statistics, and Cooperatives Service; Nov. 1980--July
      1981, by the Economics and Statistics Service; Aug.
      1981--   by the Ecomonic Research Service and the Statis--
      tical Reporting Service.   [80--644149]

39.   Earlier vols. issued by: California Division of Forestry.
      [76--640146]

40.   Formerly issued by the Division under its earlier name:
      Pakistan. Central Statistical Office.   [81--644050]

At Head of Title

41.   At head of title: State of Utah.   [81--641954]

42.   At head of title: The Commonwealth of the Bahamas,
      Honourable House of Assembly.   [81--640795]

Personal Responsibility

12.7B6.   Statements of Responsibility (cont.)

Personal Responsibility (cont.)

43.   Editor: Roland Turner.   [81--643461]

44.   Editors: M.E. Lamb, A.L. Brown.   [81--646525]

45.   Founded by: Eugene Fodor.   [81--644082]

46.   Chairman: Herb Breau.   [82--643886]

47.   Compilers: 1981--   D. Bandy, R.G. Swad.   [81--643322]

48.   Vols. for   compiled with L.J. Noson.   [82--642038]

49.   Compilers: 1964--1980, V. Haviland (with L.B. Watt, 1964--   )   [65--60014]

50.   Prepared by: F. Hammel, 1981--1982 ed.   [81--642182]

51.   Authors: Flora Crater, Elizabeth Vantrease, Meg Williams, c1980--   [81--644204]

52.   Compiler varies from issue to issue.   [81--644265]

53.   Name of preparer varies in later issues.   [81--644318]

54.   Name of executive director varies in later issues.   [82--640644]

55.   Some issues have different cochairmen.   [82--642095]

NOTES
12.7B6.   Statements of Responsibility (cont.)

12.7B7. Relationships with Other Serials

a.) Translation

1. Translation of: Sovremennaia vysshaia shkola. [81–645775]

2. Translation of selected papers from: Voprosy psikhologii. [81–649985]

3. Selected translation of: T'ien wen hsueh pao, and: T'ien t'i wu li hsueh pao. [81--646216]

4. Translations of research articles primarily from Trudy ordena Lenina fizicheskogo instituta im. P.N. Lebedeva. [81–640429]

5. Translated from the French. [82–640409]

b.) Continuation

6. Continues: Earth surface processes, ISSN 0360--1269. [81--643477]

7. Continues: Pipeline (Montgomery, Ala.) [80–643979]

8. Continues: United States. Congress. House. Committee on Science and Astronautics. Summary of activities of the Committee of Science and Astronautics, U.S. House of Representatives, ISSN 0271--3411. [80–646542]

9. "Supersedes the original loose--leaf data book first printed in October 1975." [sc81–3141]

10. Abstracts from the first National Online Information Meeting, March 25–27, 1980, were published as National Online Information Meeting: collected abstracts. Papers from that meeting were not published in the form of a proceedings volume. [sn82--21304]

c.) Continued By

11. Continued by: Ellis, Iris. Save on shopping, ISSN 0092--

NOTES
12.7B7. Relationships with Other Serials

12.7B7. Relationships with Other Serials (cont.)

c.) Continued By (cont.)

     8003. [81–644757]

12. Continued in 1981 by: Territory digest. [81--643800]

13. Continued in fiscal year 1979 by: Georgia. Office of Planning and Budget. Budget report. [81--644206]

d.) Merger

14. Merger of: Industry wage survey, hospitals; and, Industry wage survey, nursing homes and related facilities. [81--641223]

15. Merger of: West Virginia. Dept. of Mines. Annual report; and, Directory of Mines. [81--643496]

16. Merger of: Comptes rendus hebdomadaires des seances de l'Academie des sciences. Serie A, Sciences mathematiques; and: Comptes rendus hebdomadaires des seances de l'Academie des sciences. Serie B, Sciences physiques. [81--642931]

17. Merged with: Comptes rendus hebdomadaires des seances de l'Academie des sciences. Serie B, Sciences physiques, to become: Comptes rendus hebdomadaires des seances de l'Academie des sciences. A, Sciences mathematiques, B, Sciences physiques. [81--642917]

e.) Split

18. Continues in part: Quarterly journal of experimental psychology, ISSN 0033--555X. [sc82--7002]

19. With: Abstracts of Bulgarian scientific literature. Psychology and pedagogics, continues: Abstracts of Bulgarian scientific literature. Philosophy, sociology, science of science, phychology, and pedagogics. [81--643918]

20. Information formerly given in Part I of British rainfall.

NOTES

12.7B7. Relationships with Other Serials (cont.)

e.) Split (cont.)

[81–641452]

21. Replaces the statistical annexes to the Economic bulletin for Africa.   [sf82--4003]

22. Previously published as a separately paginated section in: Water & sewage works.   [82--646131]

23. Earlier reports issued by the Service under its earlier name, Legislative Reference Service, as part of the Annual report of the Librarian of Congress.   [72--624921]

24. Separated from: ISBA blue book.   [81--649174]

25. Continued in part by: International economic & energy statistical review.   [77--643341]

26. Chapters B, C, & D continued by: Journal of research of the U.S. Geological Survey, ISSN 0091--374X.   [68--46150]

27. Split into: Life tables; and, Life annuity tables.   [81--644350]

28. Split into: Court statistics, Tasmania; Prison statistics, Tasmania; and Police statistics, Tasmania.   [82–640132]

f.) Absorption

29. Absorbed: Nigeria. Dept. of Petroleum Resources. Annual report.   [81--646341]

30. Absorbed: Home and educational computing, ISSN 0743--9679, Mar. 1982.   [82--640095]

31. Absorbed by: Graphic arts progress.   [72--200970]

32. Absorbed in 1959 by: California historian.   [81--643942]

12.7B7.   Relationships with Other Serials (cont.)

12.7B7. Relationships with Other Serials (cont.)

g.) Reproduction

33. Reprint. Originally published: Ann Arbor, Mich. : Far Eastern Ceramic Group. [82--643208]

34. Reprint, with an introduction. Originally published monthly: [Mexico : s.n.] [81–641323]

35. Reprint. Originally published: Moskva : Gos. izd–vo. Edited by V.V. Maiakovskii. Ceased in 1925. Continued by: Novyi lef. [82--644122]

36. Reprint, with two supplements added: Dav a censura, and Bibliografia "Davu". Originally published irregularly: Praha : L'. Obtulovic, 1924--1925; Bratislava : Zd. Merc (varies), 1926–1937. Issues for 1926--1936 called also v. 2--v. 8. Suspended 1927–1928. [82--644154]

37. Reprint. Originally published: City of Washington : s.n.,   (Printed at the Globe Office, by F.P. Blair) [81--641488]

38. Reprint. Originally published monthly (irregular): Tokyo–to : Nihon Chugoku Yuko Kyokai Chugoku Kenkyu Iinkai, [1970]; Nihon Chugoku Yuko Kyokai Shuppanbu, [1971--1973]; Nitchu Shuppan, [1974–1980]   [82--642468]

h.) Edition

39. Issued also in English under title: Statistical year book. [81--640813]

40. Issued also in Spanish: La Economia cubana. [82–642408]

41. Also issued in a London edition published since 1823. [82--643641]

42. English ed. of: Directorio de servicios para la comunidad. [81–649138]

44

12.7B7. Relationships with Other Serials (cont.)

12.7B7. Relationships with Other Serials (cont.)

h.) Edition (cont.)

43. Also published in Dutch and German editions.   [81–643826]

44. Regional editions issued.   [82–640544]

45. Vols. for 1967/68–1970/71 issued also separately as House of Commons papers.   [sc82–5014]

46. Each issue also published in paperback with a distinctive title.   [sn82–21429]

j.) Numerous Editions

47. Numerous editions.   [AACR 2]

k.) Supplements

48. Supplement to: Anuario estadistico de Cuba.   [81–641249]

49. Issued as supplement to: Chartered surveyor, and: Chartered quantity surveyor.   [sn82–20945]

50. Issued as an annual supplement to: Industrial design magazine.   [81–642324]

51. Issued as Supplement Three to: The Book of the States.   [82–641542]

52. Supplement to: Serie A/Serie B, Serie C, and Serie D of Comptes rendus des seances de l'Academie des sciences, 1979–80; Serie I, Serie II, and Serie III of Comptes rendus des seances de l'Academie des sciences, 1981–   [81–642839]

53. Issued as a special number of: Conjoncture economique regionale, and: Sud information economique.   [81–640209]

NOTES
12.7B7. Relationships with Other Serials (cont.)

12.7B7. Relationships with Other Serials (cont.)

k.) Supplements (cont.)

54. Vols. for 1978– issued as an annex to: Newsletter (World Health Organization. Special Programme for Research and Training in Tropical Diseases)   [sc80--1441]

55. Issues for 1956-- accompanied by Annual statistical sup--plement, 1955-- (statistics for 1949--54 published in the Sept. issue, 1950--55)   [40--29327]

56. Updated and supplemented by 2 monthly periodicals: Corporate updates, and Corporate giving watch.   [82--643285]

57. Vols. for 195 --19   accompanied by a supplementary report, dated July, with title: The midyear economic report.   [47–32975]

58. Updated by supplements with title: Recent publications.   [81--649659]

59. Supplement called Annexes accompanies some numbers.   [81--643480]

60. Vol. 2, no. 1 accompanied by: Reglamento del Tribunal Supremo de Puerto Rico.   [81–645603]

61. No. 12 (July 1980) has a supplement dated July 1981 and called Research series, supplement.   [sn82--21382]

62. 1981 ed. contains Silver Jubilee historical supplement.   [81--643156]

63. Unnumbered supplements accompany some issues.   [81–640550]

64. Includes an annual supplement.   [81--646083]

65. Editions kept up to date by midyear supplements.   [82--640252]

66. "Kept up to date by supplements from time to time."   [81–645031]

12.7B7.   Relationships with Other Serials (cont.)

k.) Supplements (cont.)

67. Updated by continuing supplementary material and cumulated irregularly. [81--640689]

68. Special issues accompany some no. [sn82--20877]

69. Accompanied by occasional chapbooks. [81--644127]

70. Vols. for 1941--51 include separately paged supplement photographs. [41--27154]

71. Has supplement: Comptes rendus des seances de l'Academie des sciences. Vie academique. [81--642923]

Miscellaneous Relationships

72. A companion vol. to: Trade names dictionary. [82--642841]

73. Companion publication to: Res mechanica letters. [81--645903]

74. Designed for use with: The MacNeil/Lehrer report. [81--641111]

75. " . . . to complement the annual volume of Statutes of New Brunswick published by the Queen's printer." [81--640927]

76. Index to: Australian official journal of patents, trade marks, and designs. [82--641884]

77. Issued also in an annual cumulation. [sn80--1070]

78. Cumulated annually on microfiche. [sn82--4163]

79. Annual cumulation of the quarterly publication. [81--640968]

80. Covers the documents abstracted and announced in: Resources in education, published by ERIC.

12.7B7.   Relationships with Other Serials (cont.)

12.7B7.   Relationships with Other Serials (cont.)

Miscellaneous Relationships (cont.)

[81–640293]

81. Quinquennial cumulations include the quinquennial cumulations of: Music and phonorecords, 1958--1972; Music, books on music, and sound recordings, 1973--   ; Motion pictures and film strips, 1958–1972; Films and other materials for projection, 1973--1977 (Vols. for 1979--   called: Audiovisual materials, ISSN 0190--9827) [56–60041]

82. Recompilation of health care law digests published in monthly issues of: Specialty law digest. Health care. [82–640953]

83. Reprinted from the Monthly labor review, with supple--mentary tables.   [81–645551]

84. Contents reprinted from: AIA journal.   [81--640394]

85. Updates: Moody's international manual.   [sn81–2025]

86. Kept up--to--date by: Moody's international news reports.   [82--641212]

87. Updated between editions by: Ernst & Whinney interna--tional quarterly.   [sn82--21039]

88. Issued in place of: Sing out, 1982--   [83--640284]

89. Membership directory published every sixth year in lieu of the annual research volume. [sn82--20931]

90. Based on 1978--   ed. of: National Fire Protection Association. National electrical code.   [81--642618]

91. Vols. for 1936--Nov. 1939 include: Le livre francais, which was also published separately.   [sc82--3345]

92. Issued as a regular no. of Merchandising.   [sn82--21442]

12.7B7. Relationships with Other Serials (cont.)

12.7B8. Numbering and Chronological Designation

Double Numbering

1. Vol. 2, no. 1 called also consecutive issue no. 3. [82--643858]

2. Sept. 1961–1968 called series 1–12. [81–646511]

3. Vols. for May 1880--Mar. 1883 called also t. 1–3. [81–641962]

4. Issues for Feb. 27, 1976–Mar. 5, 1976 called also v. 26, no. 8--9. [76--644247]

5. Issues for   called also v. 1. [82--644205]

6. Issues for July--Dec. 1980– called also 1st-- supplement [82--642651]

7. Vols. for 1980-- called also 13e-- annee. [sn82--21316]

8. Issues for   called also   [81--640804]

9. Some issues have vol. designation also. [81--645088]

10. Later issues have vol. and numbering designations also. [81--643996]

11. Vols. for Sept. 1981 continue the numbering of the Federal bar news and also carry the numbering of the Federal bar journal; v. 40, no. 1. [82--641556]

12. Carries vol. numbering and date of the original. [81--643536]

Inconsistency in Numbering

13. Vol. 2, no. 4 incorrectly called v. 2, no. 3. [78--642407]

14. Issues for July and Nov. 1977 called v. 175, no. 7 and 10 but constitute v. 176, no. 1 and 5. [81--641472]

15. Issue for Mar. 1982 called vol. 4, no. 3 but constitutes vol.

NOTES
12.7B8.   Numbering and Chronological Designation

Inconsistency in Numbering (cont.)

       3, no. 4. [82--643123]

16. Issue for Dec. 14, 1981 erroneously numbered Vol. 4, no. 37, following the numbering sequence of: NAHB builder. [83--641518]

17. Issue for Aug. 1979 contains note to correct vol. numbering of Apr. 1979 issue from v. 3, no. 1 to v. 1, no. 1. [sn82--20533]

18. Issues for 1970 and 1972 called vol. 2. Began consecutive numbering with issue no. 8, Feb, 1973. [81--644020]

19. Vol. numbering ends with summer/fall 1978 issue; whole numbering begins with May 1979 issue. [81--649127]

20. Issue for Oct. 1975 also called new series. [82--640030]

21. Numbering irregular; also called issue no., no., issue; issues for 1976--1977 called also vol. 2; issue 7/8 (spring 1978) called also year 4. [81--645735]

22. Issues for   numbered GI EEI. [81--641982]

Introductory Numbers

23. Preceded by an unnumbered issue, dated Sept. 1977. [79--643245]

24. Vol. 1, no. 1 preceded by a "Pilot issue" called v. 1, no. 0. [sn82--20130]

25. Introductory no., called Edicion inaugural, issued Oct. 20, 1979. [82--642435]

26. Introductory no., called no. 0, issued Feb.–Mar. 1977. [82--640091]

27. Vol. 1, no. 1 also called "Premier issue." [81--640447]

12.7B8.   Numbering and Chronological Designation (cont.)

12.7B8. Numbering and Chronological Designation (cont.)

Introductory Numbers (cont.)

28. Vol. 1, no. 1 called also inaugural issue.   [81--644094]

29. Issue for Jan. 1982 called also premier issue.   [82--643661]

30. "Introductory report" constitutes 1971 vol.   [81--644314]

Numbering Sequence Repeated

31. Numbering begins each year with no. 1.   [82--642536]

32. Numbering begins each year with 1st quarter.   [82--643900]

33. Issues numbered within the year.   [81--645775]

34. Numbering begins each session with no. 1.   [80--645411]

35. Numbering commences again following each edition of the main work.   [81--643973]

Report Period

36. Report year ends June 30.   [81--641242]

37. Report covers period Oct. 1 through Sept. 30.   [82--643119]

38. Each edition covers: Sept.--Aug.   [81--649444]

39. Report covers fiscal year.   [81--642167]

40. Covers school year.   [79--960523]

41. First report covers period Sept. 10, 1964--Dec. 31, 1965.   [82--642561]

42. The first issue, v. 1, no. 7--12, covers five months.

NOTES
12.7B8.   Numbering and Chronological Designation (cont.)

12.7B8. Numbering and Chronological Designation (cont.)

Report Period (cont.)

[sn82--20967]

43. Report for 1978 covers period Mar. 29, 1978–Dec. 31, 1978. [81--642861]

44. Report year for 1946/47 ends June 30; for 1947/48– 1976/77 Apr. 30. [51–28478]

45. Report year for v. 1 ends Sept. 30; for v. 2 ends June 30. [81–649565]

46. Vol. 1, no. 1 covers selected acquisitions, 1973–1974; v.1, no. 2 covers selected acquisitions, 1974--1975. Sub-- sequent issues cover all acquisitions during designated bimonthly periods. [sc82–3272]

47. Report year irregular. [81--641634]

48. Each issue covers three fiscal years, with the table volume appearing approximately one year before the report volume. [80--643468]

49. Each issue covers quarter and previous 12 months. [80--642370]

50. Production figures are 1 year less, e.g. 1970--77. [81-- 640886]

51. Each report summarizes the preceding year and presents a plan for the ensuing five year period. [81--643467]

52. Each vol. is cumulative from 1957. [76--644454]

53. Each issue cumulative from the Jan. issue. [80--643534]

54. Each issue cumulates the previous issue, culminating in a final ed. for each Congress. [81--644227]

55. Each annual issued supersedes all previous issues. [79– 642649]

NOTES
12.7B8. Numbering and Chronological Designation (cont.)

12.7B8. Numbering and Chronological Designation (cont.)

Report Period (cont.)

56. Each issue completely supersedes its predecessor; 1st issue accompanied by a pamphlet describing its scope and use. [79--647358]

Suspension; Issues Not Published

57. Suspended --1978. [sc82--7013]

58. Suspended 1966–1977. [81--641829]

59. Suspended Apr./May? 1928--Aug./Sept.? 1944. [sc82--4242]

60. Suspended with v. 10, 1917 and resumed with New ser., v. 1 (Dec. 1924) [82--643577]

61. None published, 1968. [81--646469]

62. No annual reports issued for 1969/70--1971/72; summary covering these years issued in 1973. [81--649419]

63. Issue for 1972/77 not published. [80--641946]

Duration

64. Began with issue for Jan. 1980. [81--649615]

65. Began in 1969. Cf. New serial titles. [81--644115]

66. Began fall 1960; began its New series in 1969. [81--646469]

67. Began with: abril 1937? [41--39464]

68. Ceased with: arg. 59, 1969? [sc82–3014]

69. Ceased in 1972. [82--640059]

70. Ceased publication. [79--915568]

NOTES

12.7B8.   Numbering and Chronological Designation (cont.)

12.7B8. Numbering and Chronological Designation (cont.)

Duration (cont.)

71. Ceased with v. 3, no. 1. Cf. Letter from publisher.
    [80--640597]

72. Began with Oct. 1974 issue; ceased with Sept. 1978.
    [81--643635]

Omitted Numbers

73. Vol. for 1971 unnumbered but constitutes 1st ed.
    [82--642071]

74. First vol. unnumbered and undated.   [81--910336]

75. Issue for Sept.--Nov. 1978 lacks numbering. Numbering
    began with v. 1, no. 2 (Dec. 1978--Feb. 1979)   [82--
    640740]

76. Issues for Apr. 1977, Dec. 1977, and Mar. 1978 unnum--
    bered but constitute vol. 1, no. 1--3.   [sc82--3287]

77. Issues for 1977--79 lack vol. designations but constitute
    v. 1--3.   [81--640235]

78. Numbering begins in 1976.   [81--649153]

79. Vol. 5 omitted in numbering.   [81--641583]

80. Issue for May 1981 has no volume number.   [82--643809]

81. Issues for   lack vol. and numbering designation.
    [82--640973]

82. Vol. numbering ceases with Dec. 1969.   [75--642284]

83. Beginning with no. 16, vol. numbering is dropped.
    [sn81--1143]

84. Whole numbering stops with June 1913 issue.   [82--
    640543]

12.7B8. Numbering and Chronological Designation (cont.)

12.7B8.   Numbering and Chronological Designation (cont.)

Issues in Volume

85. Four issues constitute a vol.   [81--643637]

86. Each vol. contains three unnumbered issues.   [81--649610]

87. Six issues per vol.; numbering within vols. begins in Jan. and July.   [81--649182]

88. Vol. 26 consists of one number.   [81--645949]

89. Only three issues published for 1979.   [81--649769]

90. First ed. comprised of four quarterly issues, no. 1--4, issued June 1977--Mar. 1978.   [82--640252]

91. Vol. 2 has 18 nos. to the volume.   [81--645719]

Combined

92. First and 2nd report issued in combined form.   [79--915439]

93. Reports for 1977 and 1978 issued in combined form. [79--914015]

94. Vols. 53 and 54 are a combined issue, "Festschrift Rudolf Wegscheider zum siebzigsten Geburtstage dargebracht." [1--23479]

95. Some vols. issued in combined form.   [81--641186]

96. Some years issued in combined form.   [82--644227]

97. Some numbers issued in combined form.   [78--914394]

98. Some issues combined.   [81--649769]

99. Vols. for the 4th--5th conferences issued in combined form.   [80--905154]

NOTES
12.7B8. Numbering and Chronological Designation (cont.)

12.7B8. Numbering and Chronological Designation (cont.)

Problems with Date

100. Vol. for 1978 called also 1979 on cover.   [81--640941]

101. Vols. for 1979-- called 1980-- on cover.   [81--643081]

102. Issue for July 1981 called also issue for Sept. 1981. [82--640575]

103. Final issue called 1980 but constitutes final 1979 issue. [sn82--21289]

104. Some issues lack monthly designation.   [81--642211]

105. No chronological designation for no. 7.   [76--919925]

106. Chronological designation discontinued with issue 25. [73--904759]

107. Not issued in numerical order.   [82--643523]

Numbering Continued From Another Title

108. Vols. for 1980-- called also v. 15- in continuation of the numbering of: Oecologia plantarum.   [81--645733]

109. Resumes the numbering of Rudder (vol. 93, no. 4--97, no. 10 not published)   [81--640952]

110. The first issue of this publication carried vol. 20, continu-- ing the numbering of its predecessor, American scene, but it also constitutes vol. 1, no. 1.   [81--649656]

111. Carries the vol. numbering of the former: Transactions of the American Society of Mechanical Engineers, which ceased publication in 1958.   [81--643336]

112. Adopts its vol. numbering from other editions of: Today's education.   [81-643037]

Parts

12.7B8.   Numbering and Chronological Designation (cont.)

12.7B8. Numbering and Chronological Designation (cont.)

Parts (cont.)

113. Issued in parts. [sc82--6983]

114. Vols. for 1964/65-- issued in pts. [81--646284]

115. Issued in 2 or more vols. [82--641870]

116. Issued in 4 vols., 1977--1979-- [81--644353]

117. Report for 1980 issued in 2 vols. [80--647787]

118. Issues for 1974-- issued in 10 vols.; 1977-- in 3 vols.;
      in 1 vol. [79--644588]

119. Issues for 1969/74 published in 4 vols.; 1970/75-- in 9
      vols. covering various geographical regions. [80--641946]

120. Published in two volumes: report volume, and detailed
      statistical tables volume. [80--643468]

121. Issued in 2 vols.: v. 1. Report – v. 2. Accounts & statis-
      tical tables. [sc82--5006]

122. Each vol. published in 3 parts: pt. 1--2, Abstracts; pt. 3,
      Index. [81--640293]

123. Vols. for 1980-- issued in 2 sections: section 1,
      Northern Europe; section 2, Southern Europe. [81–
      645761]

124. 1977 issue published in two vols.: Vol. 1. Title/Subject.
      Vol. 2. Agency. [82--644260]

Other Numbering Peculiarities

125. Alternates volume numbering with the Transactions of the
      Society of Mining Engineers of AIME and the Transactions
      of the Metallurgical Society of AIME. [sn82--6229]

126. Issued in alternating Japanese and European editions with
      the even nos. being Japanese and describing Japanese cars

Other Numbering Peculiarities (cont.)

and the odds nos. being European, describing European cars.   [81–642225]

127. Referred to as the "all year" issue to distinguish it from the 3 seasonal issues.   [81--640960]

128. Some numbers called "special issue."   [82--641457]

129. Vols. for 1981-- called Revised.   [82--643014]

130. Jan. 1981--Jan. 1982 publisher experimented with publishing multiple issues some months targeted for specific professional interests, with the result that there were 3 issues, Physician, Nursing, Industrial hygiene, each month from Jan.--Apr. 1981, 2 issues, Safety and Health, for Sept. 1981, and Jan. 1982. The publisher has now abandoned this practice.   [82--641424]

12.7B9.   Publication, Distribution, Etc.

1. Published: Montreal, 1975--   [81--641155]

2. Published: Hyattsville, Md., 1956--1970; Belle Fourche, S.D., 1971--   [81--640864]

3. Place of publication varies.   [gpo82--9080]

4. Issues for Jan. 1976--   published in Cape Canaveral, Fla. by Howard Allen Enterprises, Inc.   [81--641870]

5. Published: Clarement, W.A. : Claremont Teachers College, 1979?--   [81--641814]

6. Published: New York : Committee on Air Pollution Con--trols of the American Society of Mechanical Engineers, --1961; Washington, D.C. : U.S. Division of Air Pollu--tion, 1962--1966; Raleigh, N.C. : U.S. National Air Pollution Control Administration, 1969; Research Triangle Park, N.C. : U.S. Environmental Protection Agency, Office of Air Quality Planning and Standards, 1972--   [81--645141]

7. Imprint varies.   [79--644567]

8. Vol. for   publ. by Chicorel Library Pub. Corp. [81--645006]

9. Reports for 1974--   published by the Directorate under a later name: Directorate for Social Affairs, Manpower and Education.   [sc82--2220]

10. Issue for fiscal years 1979--80 through 1988--89 published in Dec. 1978 by its Division of Planning and Research and again in rev. ed. in Dec. 1979 under its later name, Division of Resource and Information Management. [82--643287]

11. Published by: Office of Long--Range Assessments and Research, Bureau of Intelligence and Research, U.S. Dept. of State, June 1980--   [80--644750]

12. Published by: Saturday Evening Post Co., Nov./Dec. 1977--   ; Helen Dwight Reid Educational Foundation,

NOTES

12.7B9.   Publication, Distribution, Etc.

12.7B9. Publication, Distribution, Etc. (cont.)

[82--641485]

13. Beginning with Jan. 1981, for sale by the Supt. of Docs.,
     U.S. G.P.O.   [81--644147]

14. Information incorrect in document as to for sale by the
     Supt. of Docs.   [81--641374]

15. Printer varies.   [82--644210]

16. A publication for: the Association of South East Asian
     Nations.   [80--942334]

17. Published and distributed on behalf of the International
     Tunnelling Association.   [81--642657]

18. Published with the collaboration of: Centre national de
     la recherche scientifique, Institut national de la recherche
     agronomique, and Office de la recherche scientifique des
     territoires d'outre--mer.   [81--645733]

19. No. 1 reprinted Apr. 1975.   [sn80--2566]

20. Vol. 2 published in 1979.   [sf83--1005]

12.7B9.   Publication, Distribution, Etc. (cont.)

12.7B10.   Physical Description

1. Large print.   [77--649584]

2. Mimeographed, 1935/36--   [52--64400]

3. Vols. 1--   reproduced from type--written copy.   [41--27154]

4. Issued in portfolios.   [sc81--3271]

5. Each issue consists of several brochures in a portfolio. [81--645221]

6. Loose--leaf, 1980.   [82--643586]

7. Beginning with v. 2, current issues in loose--leaf format; each vol. issued also in bound form after completion. [81--642948]

8. "When the accumulation of citation references necessi--tates, a hard covered bound volume will be published." [81--649203]

9. Includes music.   [sc83--2058]

10. Maps in pocket.   [82--643422]

11. Vols. for 1967--   : 24 x 29 cm.   [81--649216]

NOTES
12.7B10. Physical Description

12.7B11. Accompanying Material

1. New ser. v. 1, no. 1--   contain sound disc (33 1/3 rpm; 7 in.)   [sn83–10106]

2. Issue for Mar. 1981 contains index for Jan.--Mar. 1981 in microfiche form.   [81--643525]

3. Col. map (laid in) accompanies every volume.   [81--642832]

4. Introduction is not available in microform; it is available only in printed form.   [79--641066]

NOTES
12.7B11.   Accompanying Material

12.7B12. Series

1. Order of series titles varies.   [82--643935]

2. Vols. 3–6 lack series statements.   [81--644242]

3. Vols. for 1949--1963 issued as the association's Publication no. 4, etc.   [50--13564]

4. Previously issued as DHEW publication; no. (NIH) [sc80--1441]

5. "A section of Brain research devoted to the publication of developmental studies."   [82--640403]

6. "A Wiley--Interscience publication."   [81--641271]

7. "A Bill publication" – Cover.   [82--643875]

NOTES
12.7B12.   Series

12.7B14. Audience

1. Intended audience: TRS--80 users.   [82--643857]

2. Intended audience: Biology, chemistry, and physics classes, grades 10--12.   [sn81--424]

3. For those interested in the literature pertaining to running. [81--646364]

4. For small and mid--size companies.   [82--640992]

5. Provides information for legislators, boards of education and administrators.   [81--621262]

6. "For official use only" (varies slightly)   [sc82--6882]

NOTES
12.7B14.   Audience

12.7B16. Other Formats Available

1. Available in microform from University Microfilms International.   [82--643544]

2. Available on microfiche from University Microfilms. [82--641549]

3. Also available in microfilm and microfiche formats. [sn80–11867]

4. Available on microfiche simultaneously with the paper edition and on microfilm at the end of the subscription year.   [81–642657]

5. Available also in braille.   [77--649584]

NOTES
12.7B16.   Other Formats Available

12.7B17.   Indexes

1. Indexes: Vols. 2 and 3 (1974 & 1975)--vols. 4 & 5 (1976
    & 1977)   [81--641577]

2. Indexes: Vols. 1--18, 1950--75, in v. 18, no. 3 (Includes
    index to: Shaw bulletin)   [sn82--20186]

3. Indexes: Vols. 1--4, 1933--36 in v. 5, no. 3 (Includes
    index to the journal under its later title)   [sf82--8002]

4. Indexes: Vol. 1 (1967)–3 (1969) in v. 3; vols. 1 (1967)--
    6 (1972) in v. 6.   [81--641752]

5. Indexes: Name cumulative index v. 11 (1964)–17 (1971)
    1 v.   [68--7576]

6. Indexes: Subject and author index: Vols. 1--4, 1948--50,
    in v. 4.; Vols. 5--10, 1951--56. 1 v. Author index: Vols.
    11--15, 1957--61. 3 v.; Vols. 16–20, 1962--66. 7 v.
    Subject index: Vols. 11--15, 1957--61. 4 v.; Vols. 16–20,
    1962--66. 11 v. Cumulative report no. index: Vols. 1–
    15, 1948--61. 1 v.; Vols. 1--16, 1948--62. 1 v.; Vols. 1–
    17, 1948–63. 1 v.; Vols. 1--18, 1948--64, 1 v.; Vols. 16--
    21, 1962–67. 1 v.; Vols. 21–28, 1967--73, 1 v.; Vols.
    29--33, 1974--76. 1 v.   [75--644213]

7. Indexes: Cumulative indexes issued separately.   [71--
    612972]

8. Indexes: Fourth quarterly issue includes annual cumula--
    tive indexes.   [79--644595]

9. Index published separately annually.   [83--641420]

10. An index is issued for each session which includes History
    of bills and resolutions.   [12--36438]

11. Includes indexes.   [81--643678]

NOTES
12.7B17.   Indexes

12.7B18.   Contents

1. Includes bibliographies.   [82--640662]

2. Includes bibliographical references.   [82--640661]

3. Includes bibliographical material.   [sc82--7551]

4. Includes bibliographies and indexes.   [sn82--21048]

5. Includes bibliographical references and book reviews.   [81--641004]

6. Issue for 1979--80 includes: 25 year history.   [81--642897]

7. Issues for Sept./Oct. 1980-- include section: The public journal of the National Council on Alcoholism.   [81--640891]

8. Contains two sections: Coin news, and: Medal news, which have separate caption titles and pagings, 1981--   [83--641852]

9. Includes the institute's Jahresbericht fur das Jahr . . . , 1979--   [sc82--1213]

10. Includes insert: Issuegram.   [83--640936]

11. Vols. for 1981-- include: Cosmetic & fragrance price directory, issued as separately paged section of two issues each year.   [81--643410]

12. Vols. for 1973-- include: International monographs on early child care, as alternate issues of the journal.   [82--640509]

13. Occasional issues, June 15, 1981-- include: ESF synchrotron radiation news, no. 6-- , issued by European Science Foundation, continuing: European synchrotron radiation news.   [81--643559]

14. Issues for Nov. 9, 1981-- include a section called Creditwatch. (Supplements to this section, with the same title are periodically issued separately.)   [82--640380]

NOTES
12.7B18.   Contents

12.7B18.   Contents (cont.)

15. Includes the proceedings of the meetings of the Societe de medecine legale et de criminologie de France.   [81-- 643402]

16. Reports for 1938/39--   include also the annual reports of the State Auditor and the State Treasurer;   and also the State Comptroller.   [40--28377]

17. Includes membership directories of Westchester Library Association and Health Information Libraries of Westchester.   [81--640094]

NOTES
12.7B18.   Contents (cont.)

12.7B19. Numbers

1. Catalogue 31--529.   [81--645093]

2. "E/CN.14/STAT/SER.B."   [sc82--3059]

3. GPO: Item 292--A--2 (microfiche)   [81--643159]

4. Supt. of Docs. no. HE 20.3602:Se 6/   [80--643654]

5. Kansas State Documents classification number:
    AD11.11: yr.   [82--640608]

6. Tx Doc no.: E500.7, St29fa.   [81--649556]

7. Each edition has Ernst & Whinney stock number.
    [sn82--21039]

NOTES
12.7B19.   Numbers

12.7B21. "With" Notes

1. With: Western State (Nigeria). Accountant–General.
   Report of the Accountant–General, 1967.   [81--644097]

2. Reprinted with: Nave, ano 1, no. 1 (mayo 1916)
   [81--641323]

3. Reprinted with: Savia moderna, T. 1, no. 1 (marzo
   1906)–t. 1, no. 5 (jul, 1906)   [sc82–6864]

NOTES
12.7B21. "With" Notes

12.7B22. Item Described

1. Description based on: Vol. 21, no. 17 (May 7, 1980);
   title from caption.   [81--649514]

2. Description based on: 2. Jahrg., 3 (3. Quartal 1979); title
   from cover.   [81--649517]

3. Description based on: Dai 9--go (Showa 50--nen 3--gatsu
   [Mar. 1975]); title from cover.   [81--642597]

4. Description based on: 3, 1977, reprinted with corrections,
   1978.   [sf82--6642]

5. Description based on: 1981--82.   [81--649968]

6. Description based on: Relatorio 1980/81.   [82--643688]

7. Description based on: July 1, 1972 through June 30,
   1973; title from cover.   [77--644082]

8. Description based on: Year ended 31 Dec. 1979; title
   from caption.   [82--643343]

9. Description based on: Month of May 1969; title from
   cover.   [82--643728]

10. Description based on surrogate.   [81--646204]

NOTES
12.7B22.   Item Described

APPENDIX

1.7. (CSB 11, p. 12)

There is no mention of an "at head of title" note apart from an example under 2.7B6. According to 1.1A2, 1.1F3, etc., other title information and statements of responsibility appearing at head of title are transposed to their proper position. Occasionally, however, a phrase or name that is clearly not other title information or a statement of responsibility appears at head of title. Use an "at head of title" note for these and any other indeterminate cases.

1.7A1. (CSB 12, p. 12)

[New]   Start a new paragraph for each note, end each paragraph with a period or other mark of final punctuation.

1.7A3. (CSB 13, p. 12)

[Rev.].   When following a quotation by an indication of its source within the item, use English terms for the source. Employ any of the abbreviations for the term permitted by Appendix B.9, including those that consist of or begin with a single letter. (For "Volume," use "Vol.") Capitalize the first letter of the term or its abbreviation.

In the spelling of words in notes formulated by the cataloger, follow American usage given in the latest edition of *Webster's New International Dictionary.*

For languages whose final cataloging records are in fully romanized form, when a nonroman element is being recorded in the note area, give it in a romanized form. For languages whose final cataloging records are not in fully romanized form, when a nonroman element is being recorded in the note area, give it in its nonroman form only if it is in the same nonroman script that appears in the body of the entry; otherwise, give it in a roman-ized form. These provision apply to quoted material and to names and titles in a nonroman script used in notes composed by the cataloger.

When a note begins with a formal introductory term such as "contents," "credits," or "summary," use upper and lower case as illustrated in AACR 2.

1.7A4. (CSB 18, p. 16--18)

Notes citing other editions and works. [Rev.]

Rule Change

The Joint Steering Committee for Revision of AACR has approved the following addition as the final paragraph under rule 1.7A4 in the printed text of AACR 2:

Notes relating to items reproduced. In describing an item which is a reproduction of another (e.g., a text reproduced in microform; a manuscript reproduced in book form; a set of maps reproduced as slides), give the notes relating to the reproduction and then the notes relating to the original. Combine the notes relating to the original in one note, giv-ing the details in the order of the areas to which they relate.

Form of Citation

In citing a serial in a note on a bibliographic record for a serial, apply LCRI 12.7B. In other situations, when citing another work or another manifestation of the same work, in general give the uniform title for the work if one has been as-signed to it. Otherwise, give its title proper.

Translation of: Odyssey

not Translation of: Odysseia

If the work being cited is entered under a name heading that differs from the main entry heading on the work being cata-loged and the difference is not apparent from information given in the body of the entry, add the name after the title (uniform title or title proper). Use the name in the form that appears in whatever source is at hand. (For personal names, approximate the form required by 22.1--22.3 if there is no source at hand or if the form in the source at hand is unsatisfactory for any rea--son.) Separate the name from the title by a space--slash--space.

Adaptation of: Kipps / H.G. Wells

Rev. ed. of: Guide to reference books / Constance M. Winchell. 8th ed. 1967.

Continues: General catalogue of printed books. Five year supplement, 1966--1970 / British Museum.

Notes Citing Other Editions and Works

When a revised edition (other than a revised translation, cf. 25.2B) of a work is being cataloged and

a) it has a different title from that of the previous edition, or

b) it has a different choice of entry from that of the pre--vious edition (for reasons other than the change to AACR 2), e.g., 21.12B,

link the new edition with the immediately preceding edition[1]/ by using AACR 2 style for connecting notes on both AACR 2 and non--AACR 2 records.

1) *Title change only.* If the title has changed since the previous edition but the choice of entry remains the same, con--nect the two editions with reciprocal notes. However, if the earlier edition is a pre--1981 non--MARC record, do not add a note to it. The following pattern is suggested for the reciprocal notes:

for the new edition: Rev. [enl., updated, etc.] ed. of:
[Title proper. Edition statement. Date]
for the previous edition: Rev. [enl., updated, etc.] ed.
published as:
[Title proper. Edition statement. Date].

Do not include the place or name of the publisher in such notes unless needed for identification (e.g., to distinguish between two versions published in the same year).

Rev. ed. of: 33 1/3 & 45 extended play record album price guide. 1st ed. c1977.

1/   If the immediately preceding edition is not in LC's collec--tions, make the connection to the most recent edition in the col--lection. If no previous edition is in LC, use any information available in the item being cataloged to construct a note or added entry, but do not ordinarily do further research to establish details about the earlier edition.

Rev. ed. published as: Record albums, 1948–1978. 2nd
    ed. c1978.
Rev. ed. of: Spanish for hospital personnel. [1974]
Rev. ed. published as: Spanish, practical communication
    for health professionals. 1981.
Note that the wording of the introductory phrase may vary
depending on the situation and the presentation of the informa--
tion in the text.

 2) *Choice of entry change.* If the choice of entry has
changed since the previous edition, make a note on the record
for the later edition to link it to the previous edition. Also,
make a related work added entry in the record for the later edi--
tion for the earlier edition; do not make an added entry in the
record for the earlier edition. Always make the added entry in
the record for the later edition according to the correct AACR 2
choice of entry and form of heading, as well as form of title
proper or uniform title (cf. LCRI 21.30G).

 Use the form of note suggested under 1) above, where the
title changes or remains the same, and add the first statement of
responsibility.

Rev. ed. of: Guide to reference books / Constance M.
    Winchell. 8th ed. 1967.
Note that if the new edition has a different choice of entry
solely because of the change in cataloging rules (i.e., the earlier
edition, if recataloged, would also have the same choice of
entry), do *not* make a note or an added entry in the record for
the new edition.

 pre--1981: Smith, John Henderson, comp.
    Readings in American history,
    compiled by J.H. Smith . . . 1972.
 rev. ed., 1981: Readings in American history / compiled by
    J.H. Smith. -- Rev. ed. -- . . . 1981.
In the above examples, the correct ACR 2 choice of entry for the
1972 edition would be the same as that for the 1981 edition,
and therefore, the connecting note and added entry are not
needed.

1.7B2. (CSB 17, p. 12)

 [Rev.]. Generally restrict the making of language and
script notes to the situations covered in this directive. (*Note:*
In this statement, "language" and "language of the item" mean
the language or languages of the content of the item (e.g., for
books the language of the text); "title data" means title proper

and other title information.)

If the language of the item is not clear from the transcription of the title data, make a note naming the language whether or not the language is named after a uniform title. Use "and" in all cases to link two languages (or the final two when more than two are named). If more than one language is named, name the languages in alphabetical order. For the form of the name of the language, follow *Library of Congress Subject Headings*. *(Exception:* Use "Greek" for classical Greek and modern Greek; if the item includes text in both, use "Classical Greek" and "Modern Greek" in the note.) For some "dialects" that cannot be established as subject headings, a specific language will be used in the note area only. (See LCRI 25.5D for the use of language names in uniform titles.)

Arabic and English.

Text in Coptic and French; notes in French.

In addition, record in a note the language of the item being cataloged (whether or not the language is identified in the uniform title or in the body of the entry) in the following cases:

1) When the bibliographic record for the item bears one or more of the following symbols below the LC card number: AM, HE, NE, SA.

Exception: Do not make the note for an item in Arabic, Armenian, Hebrew, Indonesian, modern Turkish, or Vietnamese unless the language is being recorded for another reason.

2) When the language of the item is indigenous to Africa and is in a roman script.

3) When the language of the item is not primarily written in one script. Name both the language and the script in language notes. (*Note:* Do not add "script" to the name of a script unless the name is also the name of a language.)

In Konkani (Kannada script)

In Konkani (Devanagari)

In Serbo-Croatian (Roman)

In Serbo-Croatian (Cyrillic)

4) When the language of the item is wriiten in a script other than the primary one for the language. Name both the language and the script in the language note.

In Panjabi.

(For a publication using the Germukhi script)

but In Panjabi (Devanagari)

In Sanskrit.

(For a publication using the Devanagari script)

but In Sanskrit (Grantha)

In Sindhi.

(For a publication using the Persian script)
but In Sindhi (Germukhi)
In Azerbaijani.
(For a publication using the Cyrillic script)
but In Azerbaijani (Arabic script)
In Azerbaijani (Roman)
In Church Slavic.
(For a publication using the Cyrillic script)
but In Church Slavic (Glagolitic)
    5)   More information may be added to language and script notes whenever the case warrants it.
English and Sanskrit (Sanskrit in roman and Devanagari)

1.7B4.   (CSB 18 p. 18)   [Rev.].

Variant Titles

A note may be essential to show a variation from the chief source title appearing elsewhere in the item. Although the source may contain more than one title, record in a note only the needed variant title, not titles already given in the descrip-- tion. (Always include in the note the source of the variant.)

Binders' Titles

If a binder's title varies significantly from the title proper of the item (cf. 21.2A), record it in a note and make an added entry for it. If a monograph has been bound only for LC's col-- lections (i.e., it was not bound by the publisher or it was not one of the multiple copies that were bound subsequent to pub-- lication as part of a cooperative acquisitions program), give only the note and not the added entry. In such a case, make the note a copy--specific one (LCRI 1.7B20), e.g., "LC copy has binder's title: . . . " In case of doubt, do not assume that the item was bound only for LC.

Nonroman Records

For languages that are not romanized, the Library of Congress observes the following practices:
    1)   *Entries filed, or subfiled, under uniform title*
Entries that have a uniform title also bear a "Title roman-- ized" note that contains a romanization of the title proper. Place the note in the note area. Trace the title explicitly if an

added entry for it is being made (cf. 21.30J). (A "title roman--
ized" note is made even if the title proper of the item is identi--
cal to the uniform title.)

    2)   *Entries filed, or subfiled, under publication title*

On bibliographic records for which no uniform title is
appropriate, entries under a name heading show the romanized
title proper printed within parentheses under the heading; the
"Title romanized" note is omitted. For items entered under
title proper, the romanized title proper is enclosed within
parentheses and printed in boldface as a hanging indention; the
nonroman item title appears under this as another hanging in--
dention beginning on a separate line. Exception for writing
systems that read from right to left: For title entries the
romanized title begins at the left margin, i.e., where each
nonroman line in the body of the entry ends; the nonroman
item title appears as a hanging indention beginning at the right
margin.

    3)   *Length of title romanized*

When romanizing a title proper, generally romanize the
whole title proper (including an alternative title). However,
1.1B4 does provide for a shortening technique, necessary in
cases of "long" titles. A "long" title should be understood as a
title that is "too long," with a more precise understanding of
this extreme length left to the judgment of the cataloger. Keep
in mind that a general shortening is not what the rule suggests.
Normally, as already stated, romanize the entire title proper.
The rule provides a technique for use after the cataloger has felt
a need for it. Note that in applying the technique, words
omitted must always be at the end, never before the sixth word
nor somewhere in the middle, and the part preceding the omis--
sion must be a phrase that will stand alone. Abridge the title
romanization and the transcription of the nonroman title proper
to the same extent. Show the omission by the use of three dots
in the body of the entry but not in the title romanization.

    4)   *Items without a collective title*

If the item lacks a collective title, romanize all the titles to
the first recorded other title information or the first recorded
statement of responsibility, whichever occurs first (cf. LCRI
21.30J). (These provisions are applicable even if no added entry
is being made for the title of the item and without regard to the
uniform title that may be assigned to the record.)

    5)   *Corrected titles (cf. 1.0F)*

    a)   *Titles corrected by "[i.e. ....]" or "[sic]."*

If the nonroman title being romanized has been corrected in the
nonroman transcription by the "[i.e. ....]" or "[sic]" tech--

nique, romanize the title in this form, i.e., romanize the title that appears on the item and include "[i.e. ....]" or "[sic]." (If an added entry is needed, make one added entry for the title romanized with the "[i.e. ....]" or "[sic]" and another added entry for the romanized form of the title as though it had appeared correctly. Trace the titles explicitly except trace as "Title"--period the title containing "[i.e. ....]" or "[sic]" when it appears within parentheses according to 2) above.)

b) *Titles corrected by bracketing missing letters.* If the nonroman title being romanized has been corrected in the nonroman transcription by supplying in brackets a missing letter or letters, romanize the title in this form, i.e., romanize the title with the brackets and the supplied letter or letters. (If an added entry is needed, make one added entry for the title romanized with the brackets and the supplied letter or letters and another added entry for the romanized form of the title as it appears on the item. Trace the titles explicitly except trace as "Title"--period the title containing the brackets and the sup-- plied letter or letters when it appears within parentheses accord-- ing to 2) above.)

1.7B6.   (CSB 14, p. 14)

[Rev.].   In general, when recording a name in a statement of responsibility in a note, give the name in the form it appears in whatever source is at hand. If there is no such source, or if the form in the source is unsatisfactory for any reason, approxi-- mate the form required by 22.1--22.3 (for personal names) or 24.1--24.3 (for corporate names).

Do not routinely record in a note the name of the person or body chosen as the main entry heading if the name does not appear in the body of the entry or the note area for another reason.

1.7B12.   (CSB 18, p. 20)

Series. [Rev.]. Apply this directive to analytics of both multipart monographs and monographic series. If the series statement transcribed in the series area is recorded in a non-- roman script and is not traced, give the romanization of the series statement, but not its number, as a note in the following form:

Series romanized: Ta chung wen k'u.

If multiple nonroman script series are involved, use the form shown in the following examples:

Series 1 romanized: [romanization]. Series 2
romanized: [romanization].
Series 2 romanized: [romanization].
(*In this case, series 1 is traced*)

Note: If the statement being romanized begins with an article (definite or indefinite) and is in the nominative case (for inflected languages), omit the article.

1.7B16.   (CSB 12, p. 15)

[New]   When formulating a note under this rule, intro--duce the note with "Issued also . . . " (e.g., "Issued also as . . . ," "Issued also in . . . , " "Issued also on . . . ").

1.7B21.   (CSB 17, p. 13)

"With" notes. [Rev.]. If 12.7B21 is not applicable, the "with" note is appropriate only in the following case: two or more works issued independently have been subsequently placed together under one cover or comparable packaging. For two or more works that have been issued together in one cover or other packaging, create one bibliographic record, applying either 1.1G or 1.1O.

For each item listed in a "with" note, give the title proper (or uniform title if one has been assigned), the statement of responsibility, and the entire publication, distribution, etc., area. If there are more than two works, cite all the other works in the record for the first work; in the records for succeeding works, cite only the first work. Use ISBD punctuation, except omit the period--space--dash--space between areas.

With: The reformed school / John Drury. London : Printed for R. Wadnothe, [1650]

With: The Bostonian Ebenezer. Boston : Printed by B. Green & J. Allen, for Samuel Phillips, 1698 -- The cure of sorrow. Boston : Printed by B. Green, 1709.

If the works are too numerous to be listed in the "with" note, make an informal note such as the following;

No. 3 in a vol. with binder's title:
Brownist tracts, 1599--1644.

1.7B22. (CSB 18, p.20)

Combined notes (see 1.7A4) relating to the original.
[New].

Rule Change

The Joint Steering Committee for Revision of AACR has
approved the following edition to the printed text of AACR 2:
1.7B22. Combined notes (see 1.7A4) relating to the
original
Facsim. of: A classification and subject index for cata–
loguing and arranging the books and pamphlets of a
library. Amherst, Mass. : [s.n.], 1876 (Hartford, Conn. :
Case, Lockwood & Brainard). 44 p. ; 25 cm.

12.7B. (CSB 18, p. 28--29)

Notes. [Rev.]. In notes referring to another serial (linking
notes), use the title or heading--title under which the serial would
be entered according to AACR 2. Do this even when the other
serial is represented in the catalog by a pre--AACR 2 entry or is
not represented in the catalog at all.
Note: If the serial referred to is represented by a pre--
AACR 2 MARC serial record, the MARC serial record will be
changed to the AACR 2 choice of entry and form of heading
and a linking note, if appropriate, will be added. If the serial
referred to is represented by a pre--AACR 2 non--MARC record
no additions or changes will be made to that record.
When it is known that data in a note do not apply to all
issues of a serial, give in the note (usually following the data) the
chronological designations of the first and last issues to which
they do apply. If the serial does not carry chronological desig--
nations by which the issues can be identified, give instead the
numeric designations of the first and last issues to which the
data apply.
Numeric or chronological designations as given in these
notes may be condensed to whatever extent is possible without
distorting the clarity of the statement or making it unclear
which actual issues carried the data given.

enero 1980--dic. 1981	1980--1981
marts 1980--dets. 1981	marts 1980--1981
Jan. 15, 1981--Feb. 10, 1983	1981--Feb. 10, 1983
v. 1, no. 1--v. 3, no. 12	v. 1--3
No. 27--no. 32	no. 27--32
1982, no. 1--1983, no. 12	1982--1983 (*not* 1982--83)

In any case of doubt as to whether the note will be clear with condensed designations, do not condense the designations.

12.7B7c   Apply whenever the information is readily available.

12.7B7e   The option will be not applied.

12.7B7f   Apply both options whenever the information is readily available.

12.7B9.   (CSB 15, p. 7--8)

Publication, distribution, etc. [New]. If the date of publication of the first issue (cf. 12.4F1) is later than the publication date of a subsequent issue, give the earliest date of publication in a note.

Vol. 2 published in 1967.
> (*First issue, designated "Volume 1," published in 1969*)

Vols. for 1970--1979 published 1969--1979.
> (*First issue, designated "1957--1969," published in 1980*)

12.7B12.   (CSB 18, p. 29)

Series. [New].

Rule Change

The Joint Steering Committee for Revision of AACR has approved the deletion of the first sentence and the first example in rule 12.7B12 in the printed text of AACR 2.

12.7B22.   (CSB 18, p. 29)

Item described. [New]. In the "Description based on"
note give the numeric and/or chronological designation of the
issue cited in the form that it would be given if the piece were
the first issue of the serial and the numeric and/or chronological
designation were being recorded in area 3. However, if there is
more than one numeric designation, give only the one that
would have appeared first in area 3. Do not use brackets in this
note to indicate either that the designation was supplied or that
it came from other than a prescribed source for area 3.

Index